Human Sense

to

Artificial Sense

How Artificial Intelligence & Machine Learning change "what" and "how" products are built

Kumar Srivastava

for Nancy, Trisha & Misha

Introduction 7

Chapter 1 9

Timing the AI & ML Strategy 10
Not a question of "if" but "when" 11
Where are we going and can AI and ML take us there? 12
Superhuman-ness 13
Simplification 16

Heightened user empathy 18
Era of dumb apps is over 19

Chapter 2 21

AI and ML are not the Product 22
End user products 23
AI & ML infrastructure and platforms 24

Chapter 3 28

Decisions, Decision Fatigue and how to Separate Execution Decisions from Executive Decisions 29
Decision Fatigue 31
Executive vs. execution decisions 32

Chapter 4 37

The New "Product" Team 38
The AI & ML Enabled Product Design Process 41
Handoffs between engineering and data science 44
Data Science in isolation 44
Product discipline does not change 45

Chapter 5 46

User Interactions 47
Types of outbound interactions 48
Prompts 48
Recommendations 49
Reminders 49
Types of inbound interactions 50
Training 50
Rewarding 50
Workflows 51
Trust & verification and humans in the loop 51

Chapter 6 53

The Data and the Compute 54
Experimentation 55

Data Ingestion   *55*
Data Catalog   *55*
Data Lineage and Transformation   *56*
Feature Engineering   *56*
Auto Regression   *56*
Model Verification   *56*
Scale out for parallel training   *56*
Model shipping pipeline   *57*

Chapter 7   **58**

Product Integration of AI & ML   **59**
Operational deployment   *60*
   AI & ML as a service   60
   AI & ML as a component   61
   Choosing between -as-a-service vs. component delivery   62
Degradation   *62*
Monitoring and Tracking   *63*
   Breakdown in the product   63
   Breakdown in the AI & ML service or component   63
   Breakdown in the AI & ML training   64
Retraining and Improvement   *64*
Integration into user workflows   *65*
Replace and Remove   *65*
   Variances in human judgment   65
   Superhuman signal processing   66
Aid & Assist   *66*
   Personalization and personal taste   67
   Planning   67
Human Loop   *68*
AI and Human context switching   *69*
Production parallel   *69*
Feedback loops   *70*
Call home and telemetry collection   *70*
Minimum Viable Product (MVP) rollouts   *71*

Chapter 8   **72**

Designing AI & ML as a Service   **73**
Engineering team organization   *74*
Model hierarchy and development   *75*
   Minor version upgrade due to new training data   75
   Major version upgrade due to new training features   76
   Major system upgrade due to new algorithms   76
API Design for AI & ML as a service   *77*

Chapter 9   **79**

Engineering Architecture and Model Development Lifecycle (MDLC) **80**

Model Development Lifecycle (MDLC) *81*
Product workflow design 82
Ideal model output definition 82
Data wrangling and preparation 82
Feature engineering 82
Model MVP 83
Model testing and iteration 83
Model deployment 83
Model feedback collection and Iteration 83
Engineering architecture *83*
Data catalog and staging 84
Data set carving and workspace management 85
Hosted training platform 85
Independent training platform 85
Local training platform 85
Model execution platform 86

Chapter 10 **87**

Evolution of Interaction Design **88**
Stages of AI & ML adoption *89*
Wonderment 90
Sarcasm and condescension 90
Disbelief and amazement 90
Acceptance and dependence 90
Starting out with AI & ML *91*
Enhancing mature products with AI & ML *91*
Enhancing AI & ML in an AI & ML enabled product *92*
Distaste for dumb or slow or unintelligent products *92*
Interacting with the AI & ML *93*

Chapter 11 **94**

Product Builder's Guide to AI & ML Quality **95**
High variance and overfitting *96*
High bias and underfitting *96*

Chapter 12 **97**

First Mover Advantage And What To Do If You Don't Have It **98**

Chapter 13 **100**

The Myth of The 100% Accurate System And Measuring Quality 101
Prolonged Time to Market *102*
Overzealous overfitting *102*

Opportunity cost and missed opportunities   *102*

Chapter 14   **104**

Public Cloud Infrastructure   **105**

Chapter 15   **108**

New Hire Training and Productivity Management for Data Scientists   **109**
Time to model deployment   *110*
Feedback collection latency   *110*
Model revision frequency   *110*
New Hire Onboarding   *110*
Experimentation in a production environment   *111*

Chapter 16   **112**

AI & ML Cheat Sheets   **113**
Top 10 reasons why AI & ML enabled products fails   *114*
Top 5 technology correlations to success in AI & ML enabled products   *114*
Top 5 organizational strategy correlations to success in AI & ML enabled products   *114*

Conclusion   **116**
Adaptability and anti-fragility   *117*
Challenges to AI & ML adoption in product development   *118*
The long term perspective   *119*

Introduction

This book discusses how artificial intelligence and machine learning are bringing about a fundamental change in "what" and "how" products and services are ideated, designed, built and delivered. The book discusses in depth, the three key advantages of Artificial Intelligence and Machine Learning and their impact on product engineering; the advantages being namely are: namely the ability to process an amount of data that is not humanly possible, the ability to detect and identify patterns not humanly possible and the ability to search all relevant signals to identify signals that are relevant and important. These advantages can work together to make products and services smarter and easier and reduce the user's decision fatigue.

The drum roll of Artificial Intelligence arriving is exponentially getting stronger. All types of signals from new magical products and services such as Amazon Echo or Netflix to self driving cars to instant facial recognition seem to indicate that we are arrived into the era of Artificial Intelligence and Machine Learning. These concepts, that were the fuel for science fiction only decades ago, are now reality and exponentially getting stronger.

We are at a crossroad where artificial intelligence and machine learning is not simply a distraction but indeed a survival event. Enterprises and product designers risk losing significance, market share and mindshare. On the other hand, careless or foolhardy application of AI and ML can cause both economic and fatal damage.

The idea of "smart" products is not new. In fact, slow and steadily, products have been getting smarter. Be it the inclusion of rules or heuristics, the path for the inclusion of AI and ML has been laid out. Due to digitization, the amount of data that is generated about users and their usage of products has exploded and simple processing that generated these rules and heuristics is no longer possible or time efficient. This is where machine-learning techniques shine.

This book is meant for product builders seeking to understand how to integration AI and ML into their products. Product builders in any organization can take a diverse set of titles such as product managers, product developers, and product engineers, led by roles such as Chief Product Officer, Chief Innovation Officer, and Chief Strategy Officer etc. Product design and engineering stands to be fundamentally disrupted due to the introduction and adoption of AI & ML technologies. Regardless of the motivation, the pressure to consider and include AI and ML into products is going to continuously grow and mandate that product builders adapt and adopt these technologies in to their design workflows.

Chapter 1

Timing the AI & ML Strategy

This chapter discusses how to determine if the timing is correct to apply artificial intelligence and machine learning. Timing is incredibly important and factors such as whether the conditions required for machine learning are present, the scope of the application is correct, users are ready for the change in behavior and the required data and compute is available.

Not a question of "if" but "when"

Getting the timing correct for when to introduce AI and ML into a product requires considerations of several factors however, it is clear that adding AI and ML into a product is not a question of if but a question of when.

In most cases, have an over-abundance of data, the need to personalize, customize and guide the user's experience and to determine the intent and needs of the user or classify the user or their usage into strategic categories or detect something out of the ordinary in an interaction end up being good motivations for investigating and including AI and ML into the product workflow.

A precursor to including AI and ML is a product design that offers the hooks that can be manipulated using the output of a ML engine. Without having these hooks in the product or having the ability to deploy an ML engine into the product will end up significantly slowing down the effort.

Because AI and ML engines require a significant amount of training (a combination of feature engineering and model training), having a robust, clean data pipeline that contains highly curated, enriched, and processed data to enable the extraction of impactful features and subsequent training. Training also requires data that has been pre-classified or tagged. In addition, a training environment is required to use the data to generate and train a ML model. Embarking on an AI and ML journey requires this infrastructure and human resources to be in place.

What is a data pipeline?

AI & ML technologies have to be powered by a constant stream of data that not only creates the set of information necessary to give birth to AI & ML but also enables the AI & ML to learn, course correct and grow in its sophistication to detect patterns and predict outcomes.

Data pipelines connect the user interacting product interfaces with the AI & ML training environment and guarantee the delivery of high quality, comprehensive, fresh and a constant stream of data that is generated as the product interacts with, services and reacts to its users.

Data pipelines enable the collection, curation, aggregation, summarization, filtering and transformation of data from the product frontlines to take the shape and form required to train the AI and ML.

Data Pipelines enable the data scientists to take this raw data and not only curate, enrich and transform it but also inspect it to generate and identify features that could be leveraged by the AI & ML training engine. In parallel, the same data can be used to invoke the last successfully trained AI & ML model to predict or classify information that helps the product advance its workflow.

Data pipelines are critical as they mark the intersection of product design specifically product interface design and the product interaction design with the data engineering and data science. Data pipelines offer a view into the real world to the data scientists who then design and train models that have the ability to impact and influence the real world.

Where are we going and can AI and ML take us there?

Enterprises and product designers need to approach AI and ML as tools in their tool bag that can help them execute on a strategy. It is incredibly important that AI and ML be part of a cohesive, end to end strategy that analyzes the current state of affairs, the product line, product surface area, current problems, users and the future anticipated demands and pressures on the users, products and the enterprises and then determines the goal and the enterprise wide strategy. Once such a strategy has been established, AI and ML should be considered as tools that can help the enterprise execute the strategy.

For example, if the corporate strategy is to increase revenue, AI and ML could be used to generate ideas to attract more users and buyers by analyzing the traits of current, satisfied users and devising product changes to attract more of such users who are likely to be satisfied. Else, if the strategy was to reduce costs, AI and ML could be used to devise strategies to predict areas of high cost and address such issues before the issue completely manifests itself and causes an incident. AI and ML enabled products, if implemented correctly, have the ability to reduce costs and increase profits and deliver higher ROIs for all users, enterprises and everyone in between.

AI & ML, ultimately, will be the strongest set of technologies that can predict and reduce churn, grow the number of users and increase the engagement of users with the product. User engagement growth is fundamentally the driver for the most important business objectives and metrics and AI & ML are keenly positioned to leverage the product data to generate insights, recommendations and predictions with the power to educate, delight and satisfy users by picking up seemingly invisible patterns and behavior nuances and using them to engage and delight the user. As existing users are delighted and value added to their experience , their profile and behavior becomes fodder for the engine to recommend and target the product to new users who might share similar traits, problems or motivations leading to product and business growth.

Superhuman-ness

A clear signal to determine the applicability and timing of AI and ML is the need for super human-ness to either understand the current state and formulate a hypothesis that explains the state or to generate a solution that can address the problem or provide the ability through a predict or foresight to a user to solve the problem.

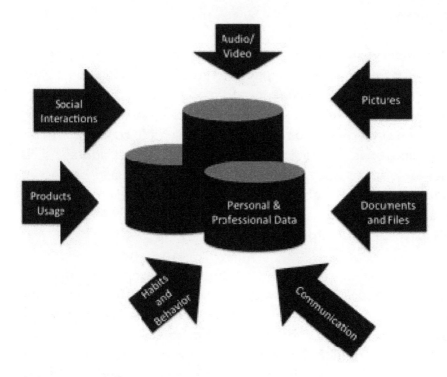

Superhuman-ness is defined as either an aperture of observation and analysis beyond human capability or the speed of search and navigation beyond the human capability. When the sheer amount of data that needs to be processed and analyzed as a whole is beyond what a human or a team of humans can deal with, AI and ML become very interesting techniques to generate the solutions.

The general consensus in the market is that we have hit all the right conditions for building AI & ML that emulates super-humanness.

More Data

We now have the ability to generate, collect and store incredible amounts of data. Every layer in the stack has the ability to create, transfer and process data be it the network used to transport data, the systems to collect and store data or the tools required to manage and monitor the systems that create, transport and store the data.

Powerful Compute

We now have the ability to process massive amounts of data with not only specialized compute such as GPUs that have the ability to massively parallelize computations (ideal for vector calculations often at the core of text, audio, video processing) but the availability of this specialized compute in a pay as you go model through cloud compute capabilities coupled with elastic and on demand scaling. This frees up enterprises from having to procure and manage massive data centers as it can be delegated to cloud service provider companies and enterprises can focus on adding value through AI & ML to their user's experience.

Smarter Algorithms

We now have the ability to process data with the constant, exponential increase in the scope and power of the AI & ML technologies being developed and open sourced. Not only do we have the latest and greatest from academia and industry available for download and use but the size of the community of enthusiasts and practitioners is growing which in turn is increasing the size of the knowledge base, best practices and insights about the how and what of AI & ML.

Willing Users

We now have users who are getting used to the idea of a smart product that knows them intimately and can serve as an assistant or advisor to help the users achieve what they are looking to accomplish. With this growing acceptance and excitement, comes an attitude that rewards experimentation and is willing to overlook mistakes as the product and the technology matures.

Simplification

Without the availability of techniques such as AI and ML, in hindsight it is easy to understand how a lot of systems that surround us have become very complex and unmanageable. As the demand of use cases has grown, systems have grown organically to support the next use case leading to complex workflows orchestrated intricately over many different interfaces, applications, processes and touch points.

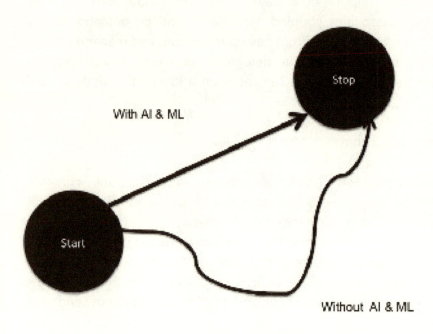

Workflows and scenarios that get orchestrated as a complex acyclic, directed graph of actions and reactions are unwieldy and expensive and often end up processing the original input into the system to generate new outputs that get successively consumed in lower nodes to determine the next state in the workflow. Such systems are ideal candidates for being disrupted by AI and ML

Take for example, the process of diagnosing a new patient. The process often involves a patient realizing that they might need medical attention. They typically make a trip to the physician's office. The office uses the patient's identification and pulls up the patients records often captured as a physical or digital file. Next, a nurse practitioner captures vital signs and stats that are recorded in the file for the physician to review. The physician then reviews the file and then proceeds to examine the patient. At the end of the examination, with the context of the vital signs and the patient's past history and the physician's own experience, the physician proceeds to make a diagnosis and the determination whether any additional tests are required to improve the diagnosis.

This process is ripe for disruption through AI & ML and other digital technologies. For example, an AI & ML engine could be trained to (given a lot of patient histories, vital stats at various points in time over their life and past diagnosis data across a large, diverse patient base) deliver diagnosis or alert patients about potential issues by executing the trained AI & ML model on a device carried by the potential patient at all times. Such a product would disrupt the entire care delivery process making it more efficient, predictive and faster.

In scenarios such as the above, AI and ML can observe these workflows, learn and develop the ability to predict the end state given the incoming original input and negate the need and essentially replace these complex systems and workflows with a single AI/ML driven layer. The data being generated in today's inefficient, complex workflows is of extremely high value and the collection and training of AI & ML over this data is critical to a business's survival.

Heightened user empathy

The goal of all product innovation is to deliver products and services that offer a solution to the user's met and unmet, expressed or unexpressed needs. For example, a system that enables the user to search for a restaurant that can offer a meal to the liking of the user could be enhanced with an AI & ML enabled product that reacts to the user simply saying, "I am hungry". The system could be trained to generate the most desirable meal for the given time, place and mood that the user currently might be in and automatically make a reservation, order the meal and arrange transportation for the user to reach the restaurant.

Iterative product development can often get stuck with blind spots that offer tremendous opportunity to innovate and disrupt the product to offer an incredibly empathetic experience for the user. AI & ML have the potential to provide such a disruption to almost all existing products however it requires an open mind and the willingness to look beyond the scope of past decisions and the ability to look at the product workflow from a bird's eye view and the imagination to dream up the AI & ML that could take the user from the beginning of their workflow to the end of the workflow almost magically.

Another cause for a blind spot on the potential to self disrupt using AI & ML is the over commercialization of product strategy. Being driven by quarterly earnings and stock prices can cause enterprises to focus only on iterative product development with disjointed local optimizations across the entire product stack. Google, in its replacement of their original search stack with an AI & ML driven technology, is a great example of taking a long term approach to AI & ML enabled product development even though one can make the case that this investment and reorganization around AI & ML probably reduced the short term revenue and profit potential for Google.

AI and ML have the ability to better understand expressions by the user of their current state and then generate a suite of hypothesis and trigger a chain reaction that can improve the user's state to the mostly likely desired state without having the user take any actions except expressing their state verbally or nonverbally. In other words, AI & ML can interpret the user's stated or unstated need and directly deliver the outcome needed by the user.

For example, consider a user's desire to be healthy as a universal need. The combination of technologies including AI & ML driven detection and diagnosis capabilities could proactively detect high or low concentrations of certain required minerals or vitamins in the body and the weakening or degradation of certain bones or muscles and automatically influence the food or supplement intake of the user (in their purchased groceries and eating patterns) and their physical routine (in their exercise or physical therapy regiment) without the user ever having to actually state their need to be healthy or discuss these goals with a physician or health coach.

The combination of early detection, prediction of a certain state in which the user might fall and the automated recommendation and orchestration of actions and events can drive several such magical scenarios that make the user's experience richer and valuable.

Era of dumb apps is over

The time of AI and ML has arrived. Data and compute power is readily available. AI and ML techniques are continuously being refined and developed and being made available under open source licenses by companies like Google, Facebook and Baidu. A product builder now has no excuse to ship products that act and behave the like the products of yesterday. Products that don't inherently understand their users and automatically and proactively adapt to meet their user's need will find themselves sidelined and quickly see their users migrate to products that offer the best possible experience.

AI and ML offer product builders the ability to deliver magic and this is why it is imperative that the community of product designers and builders change what and how we build products.

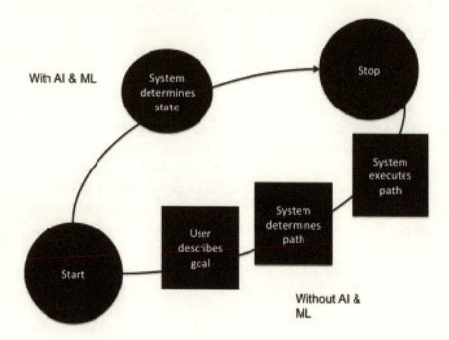

Chapter 2

AI and ML are not the Product

This chapter discusses the importance to distinguish the technology from the product. AI and machine learning technologies are not the products and services we want to build. The products and services are tremendously enhanced and enriched through such technologies but they are not the end product.

This chapter also discusses the fact that AI & ML are not just technologies but an entire stack composed of different elements such as data, infrastructure, models and execution frameworks. This chapter delves into the relationship of AI & ML as a whole but also the parts of it that contribute to the ultimately delivered product.

End user products

This is one of the most common mistakes that are inadvertently made by enterprises and product teams while thinking about and executing on their AI and ML strategy. To think and organize around AI and ML as a separate discipline or functional area is not a good strategy. This is because AI and ML are not products. End users do not care about them as they care about actual products. AI and ML, in isolation, do not solve any user problems neither do they offer a capability that enterprises can "sell" to users or other parties.

For example, take photo recognition. The quintessential example of photo recognition using AI & ML is the detection of "cat" photographs on the Internet. This use case delivers a strong technology however, by itself; the utility of this technique is not a lot. Take Google Photos; Google Photos will automatically look at the pictures in a user's camera, match the photographs against known locations and detect where it was taken, it will apply facial recognition on the photographs and tag any users that it knows about and detect any other objects such as cars, houses etc. and tag the photographs appropriately. It will organize the photographs by these classifications and ensure that when a user "needs" to find a photograph, it is able to do so contextually, quickly and accurately. This is an example of a product that is driven primarily by AI & ML but the actual AI & ML is invisible to the user.

AI and ML offer techniques to make existing products better; in their ability to predict the user's needs or the user's next action or the ability to classify the user, their state, their environment or context or their activity into categories that might be desirable or not. For existing products, AI and ML offer new mechanisms to make these products more intuitive and in sync with user's need, expectations and satisfaction. This in turn, makes these products better, stickier and delightful.

For example, consider Tesla's Model S with autopilot. The state of self-driving technology has been improving constantly. Each innovation starting with the Anti-Braking System, Cruise Control, Lane Assist, Pedestrian Detection, Rear View Cameras etc. have improved the state of self-driving cars. Tesla was the first car manufacturer to bring these and other new technologies together and deliver it to market as a new product: autopilot. Autopilot made the Model S a unique vehicle that offered a more delightful and interesting experience to its drivers.

On the other hand, AI and ML offer the ability to dream up and create entirely new products and services that have been thus far impossible, near impossible or unimaginable. Capabilities that were often left to "experts" to dictate and direct, can now be left to the AI and ML subsystem while the product can now be designed to enable these new scenarios, powered internally by the AI and ML subsystem.

For example, consider Alexa and Echo. Alexa is Amazon's voice control system that is always listening. It can be invoked through the Echo device and users can use Alexa to use their voice to play music, order pizza, ask questions and get them answered and control various home devices. This is a product that is entirely new and just a few months ago was found only in science fiction movies and literature. Alexa opens up and brings within the home an entirely new interface driven by AI & ML that in real time translates the user's voice into commands or questions and carries out the required task. It opens a whole new world of voice controlled, voice activated and voice driven use cases, integration scenarios and new products and services.

AI & ML infrastructure and platforms

The increase in awareness of AI and ML enabled products is driving the need for machine learning infrastructure that offers its benefits efficiently and in a manner that can be repeated for each new given problem, scenario or user segment. With this new demand, enterprises and product builders face the choice to develop this infrastructure in house or purchase from other providers. This is and will continue driving the space for new "products" that offer AI & ML infrastructure.

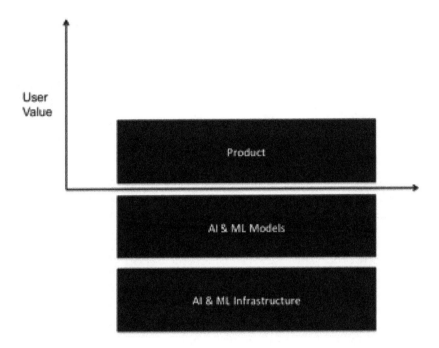

In the recent months, there has been a spate of acquisitions of startups offering AI & ML infrastructure by large enterprises that are keen to expand their offerings and services to include AI & ML. This is because establishing a useable AI & ML infrastructure in an enterprise is not a simple task.

AI & ML are set to disrupt the entire world at the scale of the steam engine. Because of this potential, its impact will be permanent, comprehensive and distributed. This means that enterprises cannot treat this as a passing fad and have to seriously incorporate AI & ML specialization and integration into their company strategic plans and vision.

Not building an in-house expertise for AI & ML driven product development is not a valid option for any enterprise. Enterprises should be actively determining plans to collect, transport, enrich, process and store their most critical data for the long term. In addition, Enterprises should be thinking about AI & ML training environments with scalable compute backed by purpose built tools to enable quick training and experimentation. In addition, enterprises should be rethinking their product design to easily incorporate, manage and update the AI & ML driven workflows.

On the personnel side, enterprises need to start building core competency in AI & ML. This means hiring engineers, data scientists, product builders, strategists and marketers who understand and can leverage AI & ML in their respective functions. Because this skill set will be in low supply initially, it is important that enterprises treat this as a long term strategic priority and be open to the possibility of establishing the disciplines in house. This is exactly what Microsoft has done by reorganizing several different departments into one single AI driven organization.

In the long term, enterprises have to be serious about "building" AI & ML in house. Given the strategic and imperative nature of AI & ML, not building it in house would be foolhardy. However, given the complexity and cost of building the internal core competency in this area, enterprises should consider a parallel, short-term strategy to "buy" this expertise. This short-term buy strategy has two benefits: First, enterprises are able to quickly launch new products and services that leverage AI & ML even though the AI & ML itself would have been built by external vendors. The time to market, the resulting mindshare and customer satisfaction is essential to keep the enterprise in play for the long-term strategy to be successful. Second, observing, working with and integrating with an external vendor supplied AI & ML technology is key to building the expertise in house as part of the long term build strategy.

There are two important facts to remember; in the long term, enterprises should plan to be disrupted across their stack by AI & ML and to ensure their survival, the disruption should be internally led. In the short term, it is incredibly important for enterprises to launch AI & ML enabled products and services as soon as possible to ensure that they can ride this way and reap the benefits of being early movers.

At the same time, enterprises have to ensure that they do not get distracted. AI & ML infrastructure build vs. buy can distract in two ways: First, AI and ML infrastructure products should not be confused with AI and ML enabled products. When delivering AI and ML infrastructure, the product builders should focus on enabling AI and ML to be incorporated into the final products. The delivery of AI & ML infrastructure, in itself, is not inherently a value adding activity. The measure of success of the ML & AI infrastructure products is their ability to power end user products efficiently, swiftly and with high quality during their development, delivery and operation.

Chapter 3

Decisions, Decision Fatigue and how to Separate Execution Decisions from Executive Decisions

This chapter discusses the concept of decisions that are made before, during and after the use of products and services and the role that AI and ML play in or can play in these decisions. In addition, the chapter discusses the concept of decision fatigue and how product designers can separate execution decisions from executive decisions.

AI and ML are ideal for scenarios that require decisions. Be it a decision that the user needs to make or whether a decision needs to be made to move the user's experience forward, AI and ML can offer the ability and techniques to make it happen. All products require users to make decisions; even though decisions can be mission critical or non critical, a pleasant product experience requires that the user not only make good, timely decisions but are offered all required information to enable them to make the best decisions.

For example, consider the simple act of driving a car. Even though most drivers don't really think much about driving a car, it is a complex workflow that requires multiple decisions that process new information in real time to generate driving actions. Car features such as blind spot alerting or swerving detection or skidding detection generate new insights that drivers can incorporate in their driving decision-making. Humans are generally good drivers after enough practice but cars still hold the record for the most number of fatalities across any means of transports and humans tend to get distracted often (e.g. a car pulled over by a cop on the highway) and these distractions often cause more accidents. Reducing distractions and reducing the number of such errors in driving is a great example of where AI & ML can enhance the driving experience and as we have seen in the past few months, almost entirely transform it.

Product builders and designers spend a lot of time thinking about the decisions that a user would need to make while using a product. The decisions that a user needs to make open new paths in the product workflows. In addition, when end-to-end workflows require many different products to be used in conjunction with each other, the impact of a decision has to be carried forward and integrated into the other product.

For example, the task of booking a vacation is a fairly complex task that requires a series of actions to be carried out sequentially and often iteratively moving from the abstract space into a concrete itinerary and culminating in a series of actions that users take before the vacation starts (call a cab, turn on the security alarm, change the thermostat settings, hold the mail at the post office etc.), during the vacation and once they are back from the vacation. In this task, a lot of products and services come together, interact and integrate to bring the entire vacation together. Each service (travel booking, airlines, cabs, home security, weather services, thermostat service etc.) has to interact and integrate with a set of upstream and downstream services. Often, the user ends up being the one connecting the dots between these products and services however, these products are beginning to get smarter and integrate with each other seamlessly and adjust their own settings and workflows in response to information received from other services in the ecosystem.

Decision Fatigue

Even a well designed, let alone a poorly designed one can cause decision fatigue in the user. Decision fatigue is the tendency of the user to ignore, miss or misinterpret decisions that need to be made or subsequently make incorrect or incomplete or indeterminate decisions. Decision fatigue worsens the user's product experience ultimately leading to the product not working correctly to deliver on the user's needs. This often ends with the user terminating their association or usage of the product.

Consider the example of email management. Email is one of the most widely recognized products that users loathe but are unable to ignore. Triaging an inbox takes a long time and a user has to go through each an every email and make decisions around whether to trust the email or not, whether to respond right away or store it for a follow up at a later point in time, whether to delete the email to save it, whether to archive it or maybe download the associated attachment. Products like Outlook have created features that enable users to configure rules that can automate some of this triaging and products like Gmail have created automatic sorting and classification of emails into various categories such as social or advertisement etc.;

classifications that users can use to reduce their inbox triage time or at least, use it more efficiently. Even with these advancements, users still spend a lot of time triaging emails.

These complex decision workflows have led to a new crop of products in the instant messaging category such as WhatsApp, Slick, HipChat, and Quip etc. These products aim to remove the fixed portion cost of email triage and strive to remove the overhead of dealing with the email products.

Decision fatigue is experienced both by users and product designers. Designing a product is an exercise in tradeoffs between an uninterrupted experience and a comprehensive and satisfactory experience for the user. As product designers work on building the workflow, they themselves can be forced to compensate for the lack of insight into the user's state of mind, stage in the workflow or the ability of the system to understand the user's intent by adding more decisions into the user's workflow to determine how the product should act and behave at each stage. This makes the product's workflow and experience more complex and disconnected and also makes it extremely hard to optimize the user's experience through redesigns and refactoring.

Executive vs. execution decisions

AI and ML offer a solution to this conundrum. AI and ML techniques can reduce the user's decision fatigue by drastically simplifying the user's experience and the product surface area. This is done by utilizing these techniques for predicting the user's state of mind or stage in the workflow given their past activity, behavior, context, environment and those of their similar peers. In addition, these techniques can also classify users and their behavior into one or more categories that have distinct behavior and usage patterns enabling the system to determine the next best action on behalf of the user.

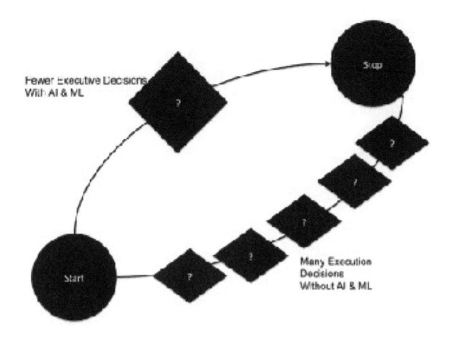

AI and ML have the potential to reduce the number and type of decisions that a user has to make thereby making products smarter, more intuitive and "indistinguishable from magic". The secret lies in the ability of AI and ML systems to predict the most desired state of a user given where they are currently. Once a system knows the state, the need for the user to make a decision or specify their current state is removed. Because the system understands the current state using an intricate set of signals and understands what the user considers an improvement in their state, it can automatically connect the dots and transfer the user's experience to the desired state. For a user, this is indeed the definition of a magical experience.

For example, consider the latest revision of the Uber app. The Uber app now has the ability to mine the user's usage of Uber especially on the pivots of location and time and is now able to create and offer pre-defined options for users to leverage that, given the user's current location and time of day and other environmental factors, can reduce the effort required on the part of the user to request a Uber from scratch.

The pioneering product in this space was the recommendation systems of Netflix and Amazon. Prior to both of these services, especially in the physical world, users would spend a lot of time browsing products (movies at Blockbuster or products at stores such as bookstores or Target or Walmart) and determining whether to buy or not. Though almost unimaginable at that time, the online experience of being recommended movies based on what the user likes and has liked in the past and the preferences of other users similar to the user has fundamentally changed how users find and view movie content. Similarly, the online shopping experience now offers much fewer decisions from the user given a lot of information is pre-synthesized and summarized through concepts such as ratings, recommendations and popularity is presented to the user by default.

From a user's point of view, this should be considered similar to delegation where the user is able to delegate all trivial or insignificant decisions to the system and are only invested in a few decisions that matter. This enables users to specialize in what they really care about making them more successful. This is the concept of execution decisions vs. executive decisions. To make users more productive and efficient, the majority of their time should be spent on executive decisions that they care about immensely with the AI & ML enabled system taking care of all execution level decisions. When users have to make fewer decisions, they have the time and freedom to make better choices because the most important decisions get the maximum amount of time.

A danger of ignoring the distinction between executive and execution decisions is the impact of noise created by the execution decisions that can often outnumber executive decisions by a large factor. Users can often get lost in these execution decisions and either completely miss the executive decision or make a mistake because they might be distracted. In addition, products with a very large set of execution decisions (imagine an airline cockpit interface) tend to have a much higher training and onboarding cost. If an average user were to walk into an airplane's cockpit, chances are that they would not know where to even start. However, at the same time, if a user knew how to turn on the auto pilot and enter in the destination coordinates, they would be able to pilot the aircraft successfully. In this case, turning on the autopilot to a specific destination is an executive decision and because of the autopilot technology, the user is no longer required to perform a host of execution decisions.

This was the same problem that plagued Facebook and the early versions of its privacy settings. The impact of prompting and presenting every single, leaf node level privacy setting that potentially enabled users to control the privacy setting for each and every feature in Facebook was incredible as the sheer scope and the time required to go through the settings was a non starter for a lot of users and it ended up leaving the users unprotected. Successive versions of the privacy settings hid this complexity and asked users to make higher-level executive decisions around privacy management and made the execution level (lower, feature level privacy management) optional.

Consider the following decision matrix for watching a movie on Netflix

Decision	Executive?	Execution?
Do I have time to watch a movie?	Yes	No
What movie should I watch?	Yes	No
Are there any new movies out there?	No	Yes
Should I watch a movie that I have watched already?	No	Yes
Are the movies in the genre that I generally prefer?	No	Yes
Have my friends recommended any movies lately?	No	Yes
Are there actors that I like in the movie?	No	Yes
Are the movies appropriate for everyone watching?	No	Yes

Product builders should think about the concept of a decision framework for their products and highlight the decisions that can be delegated to an AI & ML feature set and the set of decisions that can be left to the user with the AI & ML system providing contextual and relevant information to enable those decisions.

Chapter 4

The New "Product" Team

This chapter discusses the significance of the optimal team makeup to create indistinguishable from magic, products and services. The ideal team structure requires and even increases the need for product and systems thinking and needs the availability of functional roles that can nurture and grow the AI technology to build better, faster and smarter products.

Building AI & ML enabled products requires a significant change in how teams are organized and how inter-team dependencies and handshakes need to occur. AI & ML techniques essentially deliver a model and algorithm that attempts to determine a factor that enables a particular state transition in the user's workflow.

User and Product Workflow State Transitions

A user's product journey can be represented by two key types of state machines i.e. two unique graphs. The first graph represents a user's journey of product discovery and adoption. In this graph, the user's journey is represented as a series of states such as "Search & Discovery", "Onboarding", "New", "Engaged" and "Abandoned". Each state corresponds to the state of familiarity and usage of a product by the user.

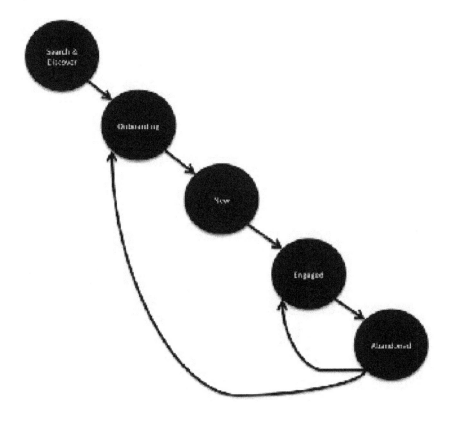

The second represents the product's usage through a series of user interactions aimed to deliver on the need of the user. Here, each state represents a progression in the product workflow that brings the user closer to satisfying their need or completing their intended task. For example, in an email product, the workflow states for sending an email would be "Log In", "Go to Inbox", "Compose New Email", "Send Email" and "Log Out". The workflow states for determining junk emails would be "Log In", "Read all emails in sequence", "For each email, determine junk or not junk", "Report Junk or Delete", "Log Out".

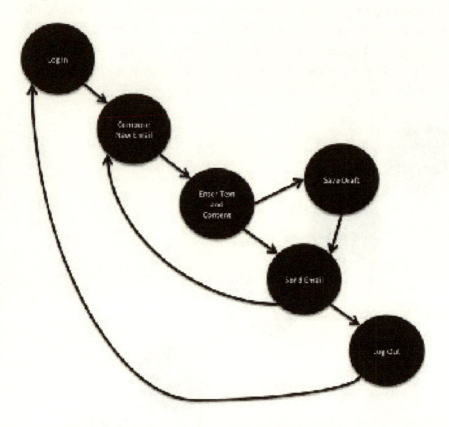

An AI and ML enabled product delegates some of its core competency to the AI & ML model while at the same time, it focuses on traditional product design to enable a product surface and interface that lets the user use the product as needed and enables the product to proceed in its workflow and also collect the before and after feedback data points to make the internal model better.

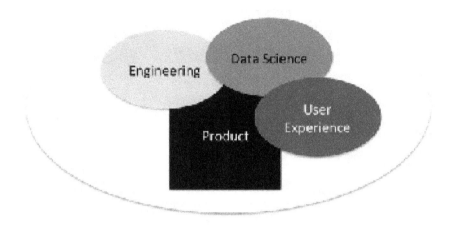

Product Team

Product builders interested in AI and ML should organize into 4 clear functions all working toward the one, single unified product vision. A successful AI & ML enabled product requires a product team that understands the user's workflow, needs and desires. An engineering team is to build the framework that   houses AI and ML models. In addition, the team needs the \ ML and AI builders or data scientists who provide the core technology and a user experience team to design the user's workflow and expose the AI & ML hooks.

The AI & ML Enabled Product Design Process

Introducing AI & ML in existing products or designing brand new products or experiences using AI & ML introduces a slight change in how products are designed and enabled. The following stages describe process to introduce AI & ML enabled products including the teams involved and the output of the design and planning process.

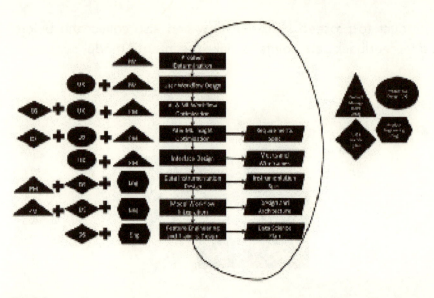

Problem Determination (Product Management, Product UX Design)

What is the problem that the product is attempting to solve? Has the existence of the problem been verified? What metrics represent a good measurement of the severity of the problem? Are the metrics comprehensive to detect an improvement in the status quo?

User Workflow Design (Product UX Design, Product Management)

What is the ideal experience as described by the users? What are the users ultimately trying to achieve? Are there workarounds or preparations users have to make before or after their ideal product experience?

AI & ML Workflow Optimization (Product Management, Data Science, Product UX Design)

What stages in the product workflow can be eliminated if the ideal information could be determined? What stages in the product workflow could be adapted, combined or modified if the product had better awareness of the user, context or the environment?

AI & ML Insight Optimization (Product Management, Data Science, Product UX Design)

What stages of the product workflow could be eliminated if the user was provided the ideal information through a recommendation or prompt? What stages of the product workflow could be adapted, combined or modified if the product could provide targeted information and insights to the user to help them make the correct decisions?

Interface Design (Product UX Design, Product Management)

What kind of interfaces should be built in the product? What executive decisions are required to be made by the user to progress the product workflow? What kind of information needs to be delivered at various touch points to progress the user in the product workflow.

Data Instrumentation Design (Data Science, Product Engineering, Product Management)

What kind of data needs to be collected from the product? How often? How will the data be collected, transported, enriched, processed and stored?

Model Workflow Integration (Data Science, Product Engineering, Product Management)

How will the machine learning and AI trained model be invoked in the product workflow to progress the product workflow? What kind of information, predictions, recommendations, classifications will be delivered through the product to the user? How will the user respond and verify the accuracy of the execution decisions made on their behalf by the AI & ML trained engine? How will the user provide feedback on the behavior of the AI & ML in the product?

Feature Engineering and Training Design (Data Science, Product Engineering)

What features are significant enough to be included in the training? What features are important for the required workflow scenario? How often would the training need to be completed? How often would new features need to be designed? How would the system know that the AI & ML model is malfunctioning or becoming stale?

Handoffs between engineering and data science

A key new discipline that teams need to cultivate is the loosely coupled relationship between the ML and AI team and the engineering team. Once the product and UX teams have defined the user's workflow and the product surface area, the AI & ML team should be able to understand the interface of their assigned workflow and begin working on the technology in parallel with the engineering team that is building the product harness for the AI and ML model. As the data science team builds and improve their models, they hand off the model to be loaded into the product harness and seamlessly switch between versions of the model. In return, the engineering team builds the ability to execute the model to drive a prediction or classification required for the product workflow and gathers the data required to understand the quality of the model to enable the feedback loop back to the data science team.

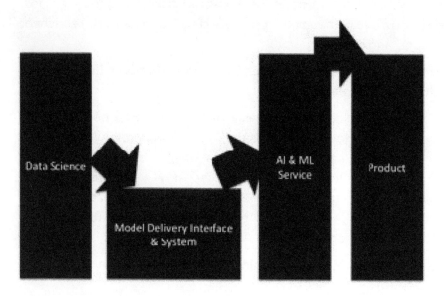

Data Science in isolation

Data science cannot and should not happen in isolation. Product builders should be concerned about creating data science teams that are not ingrained and embedded into a product team. Without the support structure of a product, engineering and UX team, data scientists face an uphill task in build a real AI & ML enabled product. This is because a successful product delivers value to the end user and the value is generated from the product's workflow and not by the AI & ML. Data science needs to be guided by product requirements and a product harness that can not only deliver the value from the AI & ML model to users but collect the quality metrics needed to define the data science team's next steps.

Product discipline does not change

Product builders have to work twice as hard to not be misled by the glittery AI and ML technology and be distracted from their core purpose to build great products that solve real user problems. AI & ML are simply technologies that are able to provide solutions for some very hard problems and have the ability to learn and improve over time. However, without a product framework around them, these technologies are useless and provide no ROI. AI & ML are simply technologies, not the product.

Chapter 5

User Interactions

This chapter discusses the key required models for designing human interactions with AI and ML enabled products and services. Human interaction can range from product and service prompting, recommending, reminding the user to the user training and guiding the product/service to get better.

The key to building smart, interactive AI & ML enabled applications that deeply understand their users and their needs and enable the product to meet and exceed the user expectations requires optimal and appropriate interactions designed that connect the user to the AI & ML system. These interactions have to be designed in the context of the execution decisions/executive decisions framework and need to establish a trade off between being intrusive in the user's experience and capturing the user's perspective enough that the system can be improved over time.

The goal of user interactions in the system should be to enable user state transitions that enhance the overall state of the user's mind. Transitions should require interaction designed especially when the system detects a drop in the user's satisfaction level in the current state of their workflow.

The product team needs to carefully design a KPI to determine and measure user satisfaction. This KPI should capture the level of user satisfaction, delight and value derived and delivered to the user from the product. There is no single formula for such a KPI and each product team (with their data science team) needs to determine their own KPI that can measure satisfaction derived from AI & ML enabled products.

Types of outbound interactions

Outbound interactions provide signals to users to enable the user to guide the system to make a positive state transition or prevent a negative start transition.

Prompts

The AI & ML enabled product should prompt the user when the user needs to provide information or context to enable the system to start, complete or progress in a certain workflow. The user provided input should be enough, no more no less to enable the product to make a smart and accurate, positive state transition in the workflow.

For example, consider fitness apps such as Fitness Pal that modulate their app prompts depending on the behavior of the user and the usage of the application. The frequency, scope and nature of the prompts changes depending on how and what the user has been doing with the application.

Recommendations

The AI and ML enabled product should provide recommendations to the user given their current state in the product workflow and what the product considers the next most positive state in the workflow. These recommendations should be easy to understand, intuitive and should elicit a trustworthy response from the user.

For example, the Amazon.com home page offers a wide variety of recommendations that attempt to predict and align products and offers to what the user might be interested in purchasing.

Reminders

The AI and ML enabled product should remind users when the user is in danger of not progressing to the next or a better state. The quality of the reminders is measured by their timeliness, accuracy and the noise to signal ratio.

For example, Google Calendar uses machine-learning algorithms to generate smart reminders to help users meet and exceed their goals. The Goals feature uses machine learning to determine when a user can carry out activities that help them get closer to achieving their stated goals.

Warnings

The AI and ML enabled product should warn the user when a negative state transition is imminent. The warnings are measured using the same metrics as the reminders.

For example, machine learning based spam and phishing attacks detection automatically warns users in most email services about the dangers of reading or interacting with suspicious emails.

Types of inbound interactions

Inbound interactions provide the ability to the user to signal to the system on whether they are having a pleasant experience and if the product is meeting their needs.

Training

The AI and ML enabled product can be "trained" by the user to focus on certain scenarios that the user finds to be at a unsatisfactory level or entirely unaddressed. For example, if the user finds the recommendations from the system subpar, the user can be allowed to highlight the recommendations that they prefer and the system can use this feedback to adjust and adapt.

For example, Pandora enables users to either like or dislike a particular song that Pandora is playing on a certain channel. Based on the user's stated preference or dislike, the radio channel is adjusted and the selection of songs adjusted to personalize to the user's specific taste.

Rewarding

The AI and ML enabled product can be "rewarded" by the user to continue performing at a certain level when the results from the product are of high quality or when the system does something unexpected and highly desirable for the user. The system can use this feedback to adapt to ensuring that it continues to deliver on similar such scenarios.

For example, Facebook's timeline uses user feedback signals such as Likes, Shares and Comments to build a user specific profile of desirable content that engages the user. This profile is used to determine other applicable content that is then presented to the user in their timeline.

Workflows

The AI and ML enabled product can be "made aware" of the applicability of its output to other additional scenarios that the original version of the system was not designed with them in mind. By ensuring that the system gathers all required information actively provided by the user or passively collected on their behalf, the system can adjust and optimize its behavior for these newly discovered applications.

For example, Google uses information captured from user email in Gmail to target advertisements to users. The same information is also useful to generate user profile and behavior information that can be used to automatically configure and operate all other Google products that leverage the same user identity.

Trust & verification and humans in the loop

It is critical that AI and ML enabled products strive for the utmost level of trust between them and their users while at the same time ensuring that the user can, at any point in time, at any point in their workflow, verify, approve, mitigate and cease any function or decision being carried out by the system on their behalf. In addition, the product should self asses its actions taken on behalf of the user as it is performing the actions or making the decisions or after the fact and identify actions and decisions that do not seem correct in hindsight and bring these back to the attention of the user. This enables the user to address such inaccuracies and improve the quality of the system.

Chapter 6

The Data and the Compute

This chapter discusses the dual strategic requirements of data and compute and how product designers need to understand and plan for the optimal data and compute to power their AI and ML enabled products.

AI and ML enabled products that are able to serve the needs of a diverse set of users who might be homogenous across certain perspectives but carry their own individual context, personality and environments requires a data and compute environment with very specific and significant properties.

The ideal data and compute environment has the following key properties

Experimentation

The data and compute environment for AI and ML enabled products should offer easy experimentation capabilities with new AI and ML enable features, workflows and ideas. This means that developers and product builders should be able to experiment whether a certain ML technique or a certain ML enabled feature has the desired effect towards user satisfaction and workflow progression.

Data Ingestion

The data and compute environment should have an ever-increasing coverage over data generated from every nook and cranny of the product line. Legacy data should be imported and retroactively organized while any new feature, product or workflow should be instrumented on day one to deliver all data to the data and compute environment.

Data Catalog

The data and compute environment should have a catalog that enables product designers and data scientists to search and discover data that is critical to designing ML enabled workflows. The data catalog should be smart and should recommend data to data scientists for inclusion in their models because of its likely applicability to the problem at hand.

Data Lineage and Transformation

The data and compute environment should have the ability to track and enable transformation on one or more raw data sets into processed and curated data that offers and enables feature engineering and model training.

Feature Engineering

The data and compute environment should enable data scientists and product builders to postulate and hypothesize and engineer features that lead to the creation of models that solve the ML enabled workflow design

Auto Regression

The data and compute environment should be able to enable regression capabilities that can detect variances in the quality of the output of the ML and AI subsystems. These variances, that can be due to model degradation due to changes in user behavior or model irrelevance due to changing market, environment or target user segmentations and are key to offering a consistent quality of service through AI and ML enabled products and services.

Model Verification

The data and compute environment should enable automated model verification i.e. double blind testing capabilities to compare models against their previous versions and other models trying to provide the same or similar predictions and/or classifications.

Scale out for parallel training

The data and compute environment should enable many versions or types of models to be trained in parallel on the same underlying training data set. This is critical as different AI and ML techniques behave and learn differently due to even slight variations in the underlying data set. Being able to train several models based on several different techniques in parallel ensures that ensemble models can be built that use the best response from a collection of models to provide the needed prediction or classification.

Model shipping pipeline

The data and compute environment should enable the shipping of trained models automatically to the real world environment where the model can be used to enable the intended workflows of the AI & ML enabled products. Automatic shipping of the model is key as this reduces the lag between training and real world application. Especially in an environment where new data is constantly being created, the turnaround time from new data collection to training to model shipping and model application in the real world is key to offering the best possible service to the user at the right place and right time.

Chapter 7

Product Integration of AI & ML

This chapter discusses the various operational models available to deploy AI and ML enabled products and services such as replace and remove, aid & assist, human loop, AI and Human Switching, production parallel, feedback loops, call home and telemetry systems and MVP rollouts.

An often afterthought in AI & ML enabled products is the operational delivery and usage of the AI and ML technology for real users in real world settings. This often is a direct consequence of the machine learning team organized as a separate entity from the product team. This disconnect causes delays in operational availability of the AI and ML enabled products but also can often slow down the design and engineering effort because the data required to build the AI and ML technology is stuck in data silos and team impedance mismatches.

Operational deployment

Operational deployment of the technology to enable the AI and ML enabled product can be done through two approaches

AI & ML as a service

Key to deploying AI & ML as a service is the abstraction of the model as a service fronted ideally by a RESTful API. Such an abstraction enables the model's verdict for an incoming request to be delivered over an API call. This is hugely beneficial for the service owner as they are able to track every API call, its context and response generated from the service. The API endpoint for the model is always up and running, highly available and this decoupling enables the product team to switch and replace the model behind the API at any point in time without service interruptions or degradation in the quality of service.

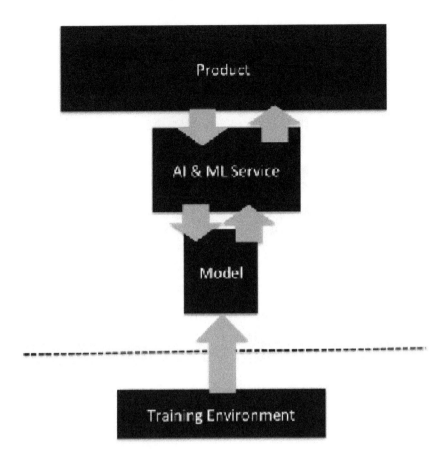

AI & ML as a component

This approach delivers ML or AI technology as either code or binaries to the consuming product or service. In this approach, the receiver product has to either build its product with the AI and ML code or integrate it into the product as a library. This approach can have a shorter time to market but also removes the ability for the ML & AI component to track its quality and service levels.

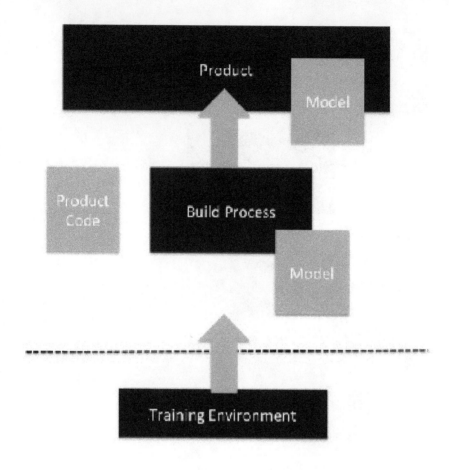

Choosing between -as-a-service vs. component delivery

The choice between these delivery options should hinge on the type of capability. If the capability does not require the following considerations, it can be delivered as a component. However, the onus of dealing with these considerations is left on to the product.

Degradation

AI & ML models degrade over time. This means that the quality of their classification or prediction goes down in quality. This can be tracked as an increase in false positives or false negatives (bad classifications or inaccurate predictions). Degradation happens when the real environment where the model is utilized deviates does not any longer match the environment where the model was initially trained. As degradation happens, the model is considered "stale" and has a direct impact on the experience of the user whose workflow depends on the model verdicts. When models become stale, they have to be either retrained, reengineered or replaced entirely with new AI & ML technology that better deals with the current environment and context and offers valuable classifications and predicts that have a positive effect on the user's workflow.

Monitoring and Tracking

It is critical that the model and its quality of service (reliability and availability) and quality of its output be constantly tracked and monitored. Regardless at the level at which the breakdown happens, the user always feels the impact.

Breakdowns can happen at any of the levels. For each type of breakdown, the following lists the best practices monitoring and tracking and remediation

Breakdown in the product

If there is a breakdown in the product, from the point of view of the AI and ML, the impact is felt in the lack of data required to train the next version of the model. In this case, the impact of the outage is felt during the outage and for a certain amount of time after the outage in the AI & ML enabled workflows of the product.

Breakdown in the AI & ML service or component

If there is a breakdown in the AI & ML service or component, the impact is felt throughout the period of the outage as the AI & ML enabled workflows are not able to provide a high quality experience to the users. The breakdown could be complete silence from the AI &

ML service or degradation in the quality of the output from the AI and ML service.

Breakdown in the AI & ML training

If there is breakdown in the AI & ML training component, the impact is felt in the product starting with when the AI & ML training goes down and for a certain period of time till the AI & ML training is able to catch up and train on all the data that it missed in training. The breakdown leads to missing model updates in the operational environment. In this situation, users experience a sub par quality of service from the AI and ML enabled product.

Retraining and Improvement

Another distinct type of breakdown is a slow degradation in the quality of the product determined by the AI & ML subsystem. This occurs due to

- Changes in the users; existing users or entire new segments of users

- Changes in user behavior

- New types of users,

- Changes in how users are interacting with and consuming the product or service

- Changes in the data generated from the product/service/ users or the source of the data generated

- Changes in how the data is transported to the training engine

- Changes in the features used to train the system

- Changes in the training environment and frequency of training

- Changes in the speed or scope (window of data) of training

- Changes in the delivery format, frequency and channel of the model

- Changes in the product/service feature or workflows in the consumption of the AI & ML technology

Any of these changes can be positive or negative. Negative impact of the above changes needs to be tracked, monitored and addressed. At the same time, any of these can be improved and modified to offer improvements in the quality of service experienced by the user.

Integration into user workflows

There are several strategies available to integrate AI & ML into the product workflows. The decision remains up to the product designer however experimentation with one or more strategies can often illuminate the best strategy. As changes are noticed in the context and environment, it is a good idea to try out new strategies as often a shift in the strategy can open up new unintended opportunities.

Replace and Remove

"The Replace and Remove" strategy specifies that key functions in the product and service workflow are entirely replaced or removed due to the inclusion of an AI and ML enabled technology in the product.

Variances in human judgment

This strategy works really well where operations are performed by a diverse set of people who are tasked with performing a similar function and are trained to perform that function using their judgment. Over time, this can lead to slight variances in how the function is performed. An AI & ML enabled product can be used to monitor and observe human behavior and ultimately create a model that can perform the same function with as good or sometimes even better quality than the best of the humans. Deep blue playing chess or Deep Mind playing Go is an example of such a strategy.

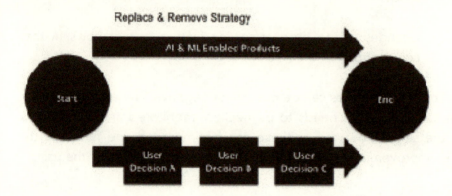

Replace & Remove Strategy

Superhuman signal processing

The "Replace and Remove" strategy also works really well when superhuman levels of signal processing are required. In such situations where the amount of data and/or the speed at which it is arriving in the product or service is so immense that a human is not able to process and analyze it, this strategy can offer an ultimately better, higher quality, more intuitive, personalized and safer experience for users. This is evident in the growing number of speech driven applications, audio and video processing applications and applications such as self-driving cars; each of these products and services are imagining a world where humans do not need to perform certain functions and the AI & ML driven products take over as the primary deliverer of value.

Aid & Assist

The "Aid & Assist" strategy specifies that key functions performed by users are enabled through value (as processed and targeted information and knowledge) delivered by the AI & ML enabled product or service. In this scenario, the user remains the final authority on how a task is completed and a workflow progressed to the next stage however, the user is provided information and knowledge that helps them make a decision that is better than what they would have been able to make otherwise.

Personalization and personal taste

The "Aid & Assist" strategy works really well users need to make a decision about proceeding in a workflow however their final decision is completely a personal choice that depends on several and potentially random factors that the AI & ML subsystem is not aware of. In such situations, the AI & ML subsystem should be utilized to offer insights and information that the user might not otherwise have access and the goal should be to enable the user to be final decision maker. This ensures that the final decisions is determined by the user's personal taste and while making the AI & ML enabled product not have to train a per user model which can be sometimes not possible due to lack of data or the cost can be prohibitive. The use of ML on amazon.com is an example of this strategy and it has brought massive revenue and use satisfaction increase for amazon and its users.

Planning

The "Aid & Assist" strategy is also appropriate for products and services that enable users to perform planning activities. These are scenarios that require the user to generate a plan of action based on a lot of information. AI & ML technologies can be utilized to process information that is relevant and useful for planning purposes and presenting this information to the user in an appropriate format and manner. The Aid & Assist strategy is very useful in determining how, when, where and what information to provide to a user at a particular point in their workflow to enable them to make the appropriate decision.

Human Loop

The "Human Loop" strategy dictates that for certain scenarios where the stakes of the decisions to be made are high; a human should be in the loop. The underlying assumption of this strategy is that every AI & ML system goes through a phase where its quality is better than a coin toss but worse than what the current human driven quality might be.

In this stage, it is important that the AI & ML system be able to observe the human to improve its quality. This can be done by having a human in the loop who either makes a decision based on the current state and is observed by the AI & ML system or verifies and approves the decision made by the AI & ML system or both. The net result is a system that is constantly tracking the human response and after a certain number of observances, an AI & ML system should be able to mimic human responses.

AI and Human context switching

The "AI and Human Context Switching" strategy proposes that AI & ML products can be designed in such a way that the workflow can switch easily from an AI & ML driven workflow to a human driven workflow. In such a switch, the product offers the user to choose either an automated, AI & ML driven workflow that removes or reduces significantly the decisions that need to be made by the user or a human workflow where the user has to make all decisions needed to progress the workflow. Having both options enables the product/service to leave it to the user to determine their current appetite for AI & ML driven, automated workflow where they lose control.

Production parallel

Production parallel is a deployment strategy that offers a non-intrusive mechanism to deploy AI & ML technologies into an AI & ML enabled product workflow. In this deployment strategy, AI & ML capabilities are deployed in parallel to the original decision workflow. At the beginning of the workflow all relevant signals and data is collected and siphoned off to a parallel installation to drive the AI & ML system. The output of the AI & ML system is then funneled into the product/service to drive the workflow.

This approach has the advantage that the product/service does not have to be adapted or changed. In addition, the production parallel approach enables fast AI to human context switching, as and when needed. When the quality of the AI & ML subsystem is found to be dropping, the product can be easily updated to ignore the AI & ML system driven verdict. In addition, this approach also enables the product team to track the quality of the AI and ML subsystem in a production setting without actually impacting the experience of the user unless and until the quality of the AI & ML system is deemed acceptable.

Feedback loops

It is incredibly important that feedback loops be established to track the quality of the service delivered by the AI & ML enabled products and services. The feedback loops need to ensure that the product team is able to solicit and collect information that describes the following

- The context of the user's decision point
- The input to the AI & ML system
- The output of the AI & ML system
- The user's reaction to the output of the AI & ML system
- The user's decision driven by the output of the AI & ML system

The above 5 data points are absolutely critical to the functioning of a robust AI & ML driven product and service. These data points offer the ability of the product team to understand how well the AI & ML sub system is functioning and the scenarios where it does not function well. The context of the execution that is collected enables the product and data science to drive product and/or AI & ML system improvements to improve the quality of the system on scenarios where it is currently lacking.

Call home and telemetry collection

Another key consideration towards the deployment of AI and ML enabled products and services are the availability of "Call Home" or telemetry collection frameworks. For AI and ML as a service, the feedback loop system automatically collects the required telemetry. However, for AI and ML as a component, it is important that the product team be able to collect and deliver all required data and context to the training system to ensure that the quality of the system can be tracked, monitored and improved. AI and ML components that are part of larger products should have the ability to call home and deliver information payloads either synchronously or asynchronously, either in real time or in batch mode and offline.

Minimum Viable Product (MVP) rollouts

Another key consideration in the development and delivery of AI & ML enabled products is the rate at which AI & ML is introduced in the product workflow. It is important that AI & ML be rolled out carefully into the product slowly either replacing or removing key functions or aiding and assisting users in their decision. The rollout should be staged and deliberate and designed so that the impact and the reaction of users to the newly introduced AI & ML can be observed and acted upon. A large and broad rollout can cause certain important signals to be lost in all the noise.

Chapter 8

Designing AI & ML as a Service

This chapter discusses the importance of APIs and model abstraction in delivering products and services enabled by AI and ML including the SDLC required to enable improvements of the technology in parallel to high levels of quality of service.

Integrating AI & ML into products is not a short-term endeavor. It is and should be considered as an activity with long term consequences in that the AI & ML embedded in the product workflow needs to be constantly evaluated, monitored and improved. Treating it as a software development exercise with a deterministic delivery can be a mistake as without proper maintenance and enhancements, stale AI & ML can do more harm than good and end up spoiling the user's experience.

Engineering team organization

Building AI & ML enabled products and services is a two-part activity. Product teams need to plan for two parallel streams of engineering and product development. The first effort is geared towards designing the AI & ML technology by experimenting with various techniques; training the models and delivering a model that can be used to make product relevant predictions and classifications.

The second effort is designed with the assumption that a high quality AI & ML capability exists and is delivered to the second effort team periodically over a known interface. The second effort is a product engineering effort that builds the harness for the AI & ML technology that enables the "upload" and "usage" of the AI & ML tech in the product workflow. This effort can be considered a subset of the entire product engineering effort. The goal of the second effort is to as fast as possible, with the highest quality level, functionally integrate the AI & ML technology into the product without any bearing or impact from the quality of the AI & ML technology.

To enable the first and second efforts to work well together, teams should seriously consider a third effort that exposes the output of the first effort as a service fronted by a RESTful APIs. APIs offer a seamless integration experience of AI & ML technology into product workflows regardless of the type of the product be it client facing, mobile, browser based, device based or server side. This paradigm frees up the two efforts to make progress simultaneously while offering a resilient, non-blocking experience to both efforts.

Model hierarchy and development

To understand how AI & ML as a service should be designed, it is prudent to organize efforts around the different types of models. The following events or changes should cause a revision of the model.

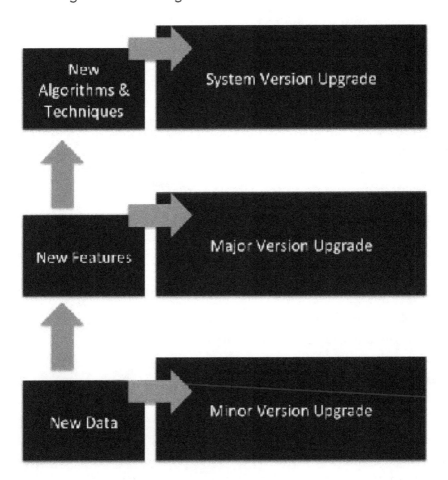

Minor version upgrade due to new training data

When new data is generated and arrives into the system, the model of the AI and ML system should be trained to account for the new data. The training window (time range from the training time to a certain point in the past) should be adjusted as needed or depending on what delivers the best results. Breakdowns or variations in arriving data can have an impact on the quality of the model and thus inclusion of new data into the training should be dependent on verification that the data pipeline is functional and that the data is deemed complete and of acceptable quality for training.

Major version upgrade due to new training features

New features derived from feature engineering being done in parallel can and should be included in a major version upgrade of the model to include these new features. Because new features can fundamentally change the behavior of the model, extensive regression testing is required before new features should be introduced in the model.

Major system upgrade due to new algorithms

An entirely new algorithm could be introduced into the model mix as either a complete replacement of the previous algorithm or added into the mix to form a new "ensemble model" that uses voting between the models to determine the final answer and output of the model in the product workflow. Ensemble models are often susceptible to the bias in the individual models and thus through verification is required before such enhancements.

Model upgrades should be designed to occur in a way such that there is no change or interruption in the quality of the service of the AI & ML enabled product. In addition, it is important that the data including the context, model output and the user reaction and action based on the model output is collected and annotated with the model identifiers to ensure that the quality of each version of the model can be tracked and improved.

API Design for AI & ML as a service

To deal with the variety of potential AI & ML model upgrades, it is important that the interface of the service that exposes the output of the model given a specific context and input describing the user state and pending decision be abstracted from the actual AI & ML model. The approach here follows and implements the principle of microservices where the product workflow "the app" comprises of several microservices, one of which is the AI & ML service. A RESTful API is a useful technique to enable this abstraction.

The API interface enables the product workflow to request the output of the "latest" model while leaving the AI & ML service to respond to the request with the "latest" or the appropriate version of the model.

For example, /model/latest/output

If the product workflow is interested in retrieving the output of the model for a version on particular day or time, the service should enable it.

For example, /model/latest/ouptut?datetime=1/1/2015

If the product workflow is interested in retrieving the output of a particular type of model, it should be able to invoke that output through a particular API call that references the appropriate model by specifying the type in its invocation.

For example, /model/latest/output?type=rnn

In addition to the RESTful interface and contract, other typical service considerations such as availability, resiliency, redundancy, performance, security and auditability are required and should be implemented as being done for all other services being consumed in the product workflow.

Chapter 9

Engineering Architecture and Model Development Lifecycle (MDLC)

This chapter discusses the AI & ML engineering platform and how product teams can build and develop AI/ML with agility and efficiency including how to organize engineering activities (issue tracking, source controls and agility)

The ideal engineering architecture for data scientists working on AI & ML enabled products should answer the following questions and needs for the data scientists and product builders

- What data do I have to build my model?
- Where is the data I need?
- What does it look like?
- How do I get access to this data?
- What capabilities does the platform have to speed my machine learning?
- How can I test my model on new, real data?
- How can I deploy my model into production?

Model Development Lifecycle (MDLC)

The model development lifecycle includes the following key stages

Product workflow design

At this stage, the product designers specify the product design and the workflow along with the workflow stages and the associated decisions and information required along with the logic required to progress in the workflow.

Ideal model output definition

At this stage, the model specification is defined to describe the answers or information required from the model for each key workflow stage. In addition to the output of the model, the specification includes the information that is passed into the model to help it make the decision or provide the needed information including the user, context, environment and the current stage in the workflow.

Data wrangling and preparation

At this stage, the data scientists determine the algorithms to convert raw data into processed, enriched, formatted, curated and normalized data that is read for feature engineering and training. The data scientist has to determine whether the data is in the correct format for them to train a machine-learning model. For example, if the data is numbers, are all numeric attributes on the same scale and normalized. If the data is documents, should excess words be removed and discarded and show the document be converted into unigrams or bigrams. If the data is a set of images, should the images be pixelated and vectorized. If the data is audio and video, should it be transcribed and/or pixelated.

Feature engineering

At this stage, the data scientists experiment with the data to define and extract features that show potential of building a model that can accurately perform the required predictions, classifications or generate the information that can drive the product workflow.

Model MVP

At this stage, the data scientists create and publish a model MVP that attempts to provide the required information and/or predictions and classifications.

Model testing and iteration

Once the model MVP has been completed, it has to be tested for quality, mistakes, over fitting, under fitting and any biases. Testing reveals areas of improvement that can be addressed through more training data, more features or configuration updates of the algorithms being used in the model. Model testing and iteration occurs until the quality has been addressed to the desired levels.

Model deployment

Once the model is had been tested to be at the desired quality levels, it is ready to be deployed. At this stage, the model is hooked up to the product workflow at the earlier specified stages and decision points.

Model feedback collection and Iteration

At this stage, the model is live in production active in product workflow. Each time the model is exercised, the request, the context of the request, the model's verdict and the user's reaction to it is captured and fed back into the system to enable a new training iteration to correct any mistakes and improve the quality.

Engineering architecture

A dedicated and long-term strategy for building AI & ML products requires the commitment to an engineering architecture that is conducive to efficient AI & ML development. Efficiency of AI & ML development is defined as the time it takes from the inception of the idea of an AI & ML enabled product to the time when the AI & ML is deployed into the product workflow to be used by real users. The goal of the engineering architecture is to enable data scientists and product builders to find the data they need, hypothesize, experiment with it, process it, build models, test and ship them as fast as possible and have the tools they need to measure and increase the quality of their models.

The engineering architecture for data science needs to ensure that data scientists are productive and efficient. To ensure that data scientists and product designers are highly productive, the architecture should offer the following capabilities.

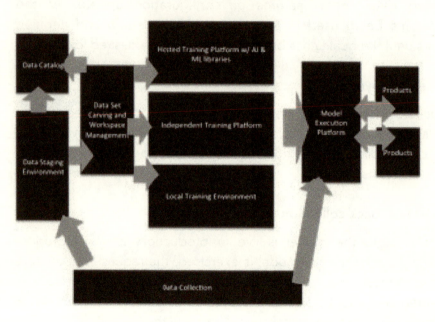

Data catalog and staging

All available data should be cataloged and organized into categories. The data should be described so that data scientists and product builders can list all available data, search and discover data and procure access to the data.

In addition, the data scientist should have the ability to stage data that they import into the system to enable a standard mechanism and location to import and stage data for further downstream analysis.

Data set carving and workspace management

The architecture should enable capabilities that allow the data scientist to carve their data into training, test and cross validation sets in addition to creating samples. In addition, the data scientists should have access to a project specific workspace where they can get access to their own copy of the data that interests them.

Hosted training platform

The architecture should enable the data scientist to use the AI & ML capabilities exposed and enabled as hosted capabilities on the platform. These capabilities offer AI & ML algorithms pre programmed and accessible as either libraries or services to be utilized for training models.

Independent training platform

The architecture should enable the data scientists to export the data into their independent training platform such as clustered, parallelized hardware. The architecture offers data export or copy capabilities to enable training in the independent training platform where the data scientist has broad control in how, when and what training they want to perform towards the generation of their model.

Local training platform

The architecture should enable the data scientists to export the data to a local training platform such as their laptop in a manner similar to the Independent Training Platform. The intent is to offer maximum flexibility to the data scientist to generate their models.

Model execution platform

The architecture should offer a model execution platform where the trained model can be invoked by the product workflow to generate an output that can utilized to progress the product workflow, The execution environment should be easily accessible from the training environment and from the product workflow for easy model publishing and model access. The model execution platform should offer high service availability, security, logging, auditability and a feedback loop.

Chapter 10

Evolution of Interaction Design

This chapter discusses what product designers can expect as AI and ML enabled product and services become more pervasive and acceptable. As humans learn to adjust and adapt, the designs of such products will become more intuitive and the current objections that users might have about these technologies will give way to a whole new understanding, acceptance and dependence on these AI and ML enabled products and services.

Stages of AI & ML adoption

AI & ML enabled product adoption is most likely to happen when the technology value is presented in a non-intrusive, product focused, use case oriented fashion. Products that tout the availability of the technology as their main selling point might get early adoption due to the initial euphoria around the technology but tend to struggle in the long term in retaining and growing their user base. AI & ML technology has the ability to provide almost a magical experience when embedded at the right points in the user's workflow. Product designers have to constantly tradeoff between over and under use of AI & ML technology. Under use leaves potential value on the table whereas overuse has the risk of sub par quality and driving confusion in the minds of the users as they struggle to determine the value from the product.

Adoption of AI & ML has the following key stages:

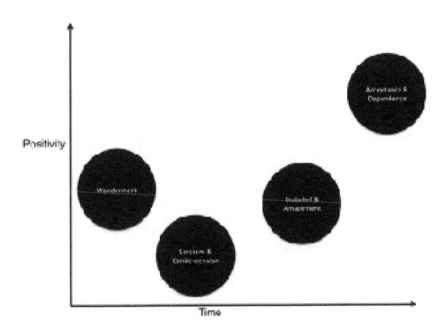

Wonderment

The first time AI & ML enabled products or workflows are introduced to users, it is often met with a sense of wonder from the users who attempt to understand how the scenario or product is even possible. This wonderment is rooted in how seemingly impossible the promise of the product might have been.

Sarcasm and condescension

As the quality of AI & ML varies and iteratively attempts to improve, users might treat it with sarcasm and condescension. Watching a struggling product or technology, users might feel let down by the broken promises and under-delivered value and might treat the entire product and the idea behind it as something that was not possible in the first place.

Disbelief and amazement

After the gestation period of the AI & ML, users begin to find the value that was initially promised and as the quality of the product improves and becomes more consistent, the sarcasm of the previous stage is replaced by a sense of amazement. Positive network effects can take place at this point and glowing, positive reviews lead to a snowball effect causing increased usage of the product, which leads to the AI & ML becoming savvier and delivering even higher value.

Acceptance and dependence

This is the last stage in the adoption of AI & ML enabled products. In this stage, the AI & ML enabled workflows merge into the product workflow and users accept it as table stakes and omnipresent. At this stage, the product workflow and its AI & ML engine become one single product working together to drive user value. At this point, due to the sustained, consistent high levels of quality and value, users being to depend on the product and passionately voice their frustration if they experience a breakdown in the product or service with a sense of entitlement.

Starting out with AI & ML

For product builders starting out with the idea of building new AI & ML enabled products or introducing AI & ML into their current product workflow, it is important that they maintain the focus on product design and product definition. Having a well-defined product surface area with optimal interactions and touch points is of the utmost importance and non negotiable. A product can be successful without AI & ML but AI & ML can never be successful unless delivered as part of a well thought out and designed product that solves real user problems.

Product designers should consciously choose their strategy; "Replace and remove" vs. "Aid and Assist". Once the strategy has been chosen based on the one that promises to add the most value for the user, product builders should focus on parallelizing the product engineering and AI & ML engineering efforts.

Early version of AI & ML enabled products should always keep in mind three important considerations. First, the system should be transparent to the users about the use of AI & ML in the product and offer insights into how the user's data is being used to drive the ML. Second, users should be given the choice to opt out or ignore the AI & ML scenarios in case they find those parts lacking. Third, users should have the ability to instantly provide feedback about their experience and what, if anything could have made it better. At the same time, the product should be designed to actively collect all relevant information and data to provide context to their analysis.

Enhancing mature products with AI & ML

For product builders looking to enhance mature products with AI & ML, careful considerations are required to not confuse, alienate and disorient current users. The product should offer a self-selected introduction to the new AI & ML driven capabilities and support the "production parallel" mode for a certain amount of time to enable users to switch between the two modes as they learn and orient themselves. In the case of a "replace & remove" strategy, users should be offered the choice to try out the parallel AI & ML enabled workflow. For the "Aid & assist" strategy, the information or recommendations from the AI & ML subsystem should be offered in a non-intrusive flow alongside the actual workflow in the product.

Enhancing AI & ML in an AI & ML enabled product

For product builders looking to enhance the quality, sophistication and usage of AI & ML in an already AI & ML enabled product, considerations are slightly different. Upgrading the AI & ML in an existing product can lead to a higher quality of output that improves the user's experience or increasing the overall percentage of incorrect outputs while increase the quality of the correct outputs thus making the quality deficiency more pronounced when encountered by the user. In addition, upgrades can also lead to the illumination of new or existing gaps in the AI & ML technologies capability to provide good outputs and change or even deprecate the technologies ability to service a certain class of scenarios successfully.

Upgrading the AI & ML in a product especially a mature product not only requires extensive testing for possible regressions and quality but also for changes in scenarios and workflows supported by the technology. In addition, a robust feedback pipeline is required to detect such changes and the impact on user satisfaction.

Distaste for dumb or slow or unintelligent products

The most significant impact of an evolving AI & ML product is its potential to completely reset the user's experience with the product and service. This, though inevitable, needs to be planned for and consciously addressed. Product designers should keep in mind that users who get used to a certain level of magic in their products not only expect a consistent level of magic across their product workflow but expect it at a consistent level every time and lose any appreciation for product workflows or scenarios that does not use what it knows about the user and their goals to make the scenario smarter and more intuitive. Users might or might not know that there is AI & ML powering the magic in their workflow but they will notice the difference if that technology were to stop functioning.

Interacting with the AI & ML

As the AI & ML becomes an integral force behind the product, it can begin to understand each and every user individually and intimately. In addition, each and every user can also begin to expect a personalized presence to know them, guide them and inform them of what is important to the user. As this happens, product designers need to understand that users will eventually need to interact with the AI & ML directly. Interactions with the AI & ML primarily will be centered around enabling the AI & ML to better understand the user and enabling the user to "Train" the AI & ML to understand them better, predict their needs in the context of the user's goals and context.

Chapter 11

Product Builder's Guide to AI & ML Quality

This chapter describes how product builders and data scientists can understand, improve and enhance the quality of their AI and ML models and the AI & ML enabled products and services.

Product builders have the responsibility to ensure that the AI & ML enabled in their products and services offers the best possible quality in experience to their users. Some considerations to detect and address in this technology are

High variance and overfitting

This occurs when the model overfits or exhibits high levels of variance in the output of the model. In such situations, the model ends up treating noise in the data as signals and exhibits high sensitivity to the data and patterns in the training data set even though it might be random or insignificant noise.

Dealing with high variance and overfitting requires that more data be included in the training process or reducing the number of features being used to train the model (among other things)

High bias and underfitting

This occurs when the model under fits or exhibits high levels of bias in the output of the model. In such situations, the model is not able to uncover all patterns and relationships from the training data.

Dealing with high bias and underfitting requires the development and usage of additional features, reducing the size of the data and training examples among other things.

Chapter 12

First Mover Advantage And What To Do If You Don't Have It

This chapter discusses the importance of the first mover advantage and how it can help products gain market share and traction. However, when such advantage is not there, the chapter discusses what products can do to still gain share and user delight.

For product builders starting out on their AI & ML journey, competing with an already established competitor production that has these capabilities already baked in can be daunting. This is because an early head start in AI & ML inclusion into products can give a first mover advantage to the product builder. The cost of setting up an AI & ML enabled product both in the product and the backend can be significant and the sooner the engineering architecture and team organization for building an AI & ML enabled product has been established, the first mover advantage begins to take shape. The faster the AI & ML enabled product can be delivered to users and the sooner their interaction with the product and feedback about it is captured and used to improve the AI & ML, the more advantage is accrued.

In addition, first mover advantage is strengthened by all the data that is collected and made available to the training system. Because the generation of data is a function of users, usage and the instrumentation quality and the longer the product has been in existence, more data is created; products that have been in the hands of users for a longer period of time automatically have a large first movers advantage.

Product builders, who do not have the first mover's advantage, should consider breaking new ground in terms of the product workflow or scenario that is enhanced using AI & ML technologies. The goal should be two fold. First, to be able to introduce an AI & ML enabled workflow as soon as possible to real users using the product and second, to pick scenarios for disrupting through AI & ML that have been ignored or simply lower in priority for competitor products. A focus on untapped scenarios can be used to reduce the impact of the first movers' advantage.

Chapter 13

The Myth of The 100% Accurate System And Measuring Quality

This chapter discusses the trap that befalls products that shoot for 100% accurate AI & ML subsystems. Quest for 100% accuracy for an AI & ML subsystem can cause a multitude of issues for the product.

A cultural problem that product builders striving to add AI & ML into their product workflows face is the demand for AI & ML that is 100% accurate each and every time it is invoked. This is especially true in cases for machine learning and AI has been pitched as magic that can magically solve all product workflow issues. This usually stems from an imperfect understanding or application of AI & ML. Some implications of this are:

Prolonged Time to Market

A drive to build a 100% accurate AI & ML technology can prolong the time to production deployment of the AI & ML enabled product and this delay in getting the product in the hands of the users can loose the first movers advantage, increase the cost of development and risk a changing market or user base that renders the product dead on arrival.

Overzealous overfitting

The drive to build a 100% accurate AI & ML technology can lead to a AI & ML model that over fits to the data it is trained on thus showing a 100% accuracy on the data set that it has been trained on but can fail miserably in the real world on new data. This leads to wasted time and resources and a very disappointed user base.

Opportunity cost and missed opportunities

Another drawback of the drive to create a 100% accurate AI & ML technology is the opportunity cost of building a second or third AI & ML model that addresses a new, yet to be disrupted product workflow or experiment and invest in an entirely new major version upgrade of the model that ironically could be more accurate than the current version. This drive can also cost the resources required to improve the model after soliciting production feedback, which is blocked by the attempt to build a 100% accurate model before putting it in the hands of real users.

Chapter 14

Public Cloud Infrastructure

This chapter discusses considerations on how to choose a public cloud provider vs. building the capability in house and how to think about other build vs. buy decisions.

For product builders looking to add AI & ML enabled products, they have a choice to invest in AI & ML infrastructure in house or leverage infrastructure offered as a service by third party cloud providers or buy tools and capabilities from vendors to setup the infrastructure in house. There is a tight correlation between successful digital native companies and in house investment in AI & ML infrastructure.

This can be a tricky decisions and setting up the infrastructure in house is obviously an expensive affair; the cost to hire good data scientists, the cost to hire good data engineers to build and/or setup the infrastructure can easily get very big. At the same time, setting up the infrastructure and teams to manage, operate and use the infrastructure is not a guarantee of value generation because the path to value is often not a straight line but fraught with false starts, local failures and roadblocks.

The approach that works best is to parallelize the operation by freeing up the data scientists to begin building the model while in parallel getting a team of data engineers to commence work on the engineering architecture. In the roadmap for the engineering architecture, the problems to solve before other are the ones of enabling access to any and all data to data scientists and enabling data scientists to run their model in the real world to produce data and insights that help them improve the quality of the model.

The strategy also depends on the stage of the company building the product. Start-ups should build in the ability to experiment with ML & AI models into their new stacks. Because cash flow is important to startups, investing a huge amount of money in the infrastructure might not be the ideal choice. On the other add, large enterprises might be more concerned with time to market and could outsource all of the platform or at least, large chunks of it to third party vendors.

While outsourcing infrastructure requirements to third party vendors, product builders should keep an eye on the integration costs and do the due diligence to connect the third party products and infrastructure to their products data generation pipelines and deliver the output of the training exercise to the product enabled workflow

Chapter 15

New Hire Training and Productivity Management for Data Scientists

This chapter discusses considerations in how to train new hires and make new and existing data scientists, data engineers and product builders productive, efficient and innovative.

To understand data science and AI & ML enabled product engineering efficiency, it is important to track certain key metrics.

Time to model deployment

Time take to design, build, train and deploy a model into product that is in the hands of actual users starting from the time when the AI & ML designed scenario is specified. The goal should be to reduce this time.

Feedback collection latency

Time taken to collect actual product usage data, context, user's reaction and action and feedback about the AI & ML and include it in the generation of new model versions. This time should be minimized as much as possible and automated as much as possible.

Model revision frequency

The number of iterations leading to new minor and major versions of the AI & ML model and/or the AI & ML system itself.

The goal of product leaders should include tracking the above KPIs and ensuring that the KPIs are improved regularly and passionately. Productive data scientists are happy scientists.

New Hire Onboarding

It is critical that new hires to the product team (regardless of their experience) be able to swiftly understand the data, the current state of the AI & ML service and determine what needs to be done next given their evaluation of the current state. To enable new hires to reach high levels of productivity and innovation, it is important that they get a lay of the land (the available data and previous versions of the AI & ML models including the code behind these models) and a workspace in an environment that offers cheap and risk free experimentation with new hypothesis and theories.

The engineering architecture should have a sandbox environment where new hires can experiment and inspect data, code, user feedback and interact with early versions of the product. The environment should recommend data sets and models to new hires based on their affiliations, target focus areas and other contextual factors.

New hire productivity in data science should be measured using the "Time to new model deployment" metric which is the time taken for a new hire to deploy a new experimental version of an AI or ML into the product workflow. Apart from an environment that enables experimentation and analysis, other factors that impact this metric include automation of data wrangling to produce high quality, enriched, ready to be trained on data, tooling to enable the "Forking" of model code and tooling that enables automatic rating, ranking and testing of trained models.

Experimentation in a production environment

A unique feature of successful products and services with agile product teams is the availability of infrastructure and the freedom and support to experiment with ideas in a production environment with real users. The ability to run experiments in production on a purpose built platform ensures not only fast testing of hypothesis to enable the "fail fast" strategy but also enables automatic data collection from the experiment along with experiment analysis making it extremely easy for the team to recognize good ideas and discard bad ones.

Chapter 16

AI & ML Cheat Sheets

This chapter lists some cheat sheets that product builders can use to build and manage user delighting AI & ML enabled products.

Top 10 reasons why AI & ML enabled products fails

1. Product focus is absent
2. AI & ML is touted as the product, not the enabling technology
3. Data is not ready or worse, available
4. AI & ML training infrastructure is missing or has a high cost of onboarding
5. The product or service is not designed to consume a AI & ML model
6. The trained AI & ML model can not be deployed in production
7. The trained AI & ML model is of inferior quality either underfitting or overfitting to the data
8. Feedback loops from the product and its users to the data science team are missing or poorly functioning.
9. The AI & ML team is not integrated into the product team.
10. The product team fails to understand how and where AI & ML can be used to disrupt the existing state of the art.

Top 5 technology correlations to success in AI & ML enabled products

1. APIs
2. Automation
3. Open source AI & ML libraries
4. Data lakes and repositories
5. High performance, parallelized hardware

Top 5 organizational strategy correlations to success in AI & ML enabled products

1. Product teams with product designers, engineers and data scientists
2. Investment into AI & ML infrastructure and team
3. Focus on experimentation, iterative analysis and agility
4. Investment in APIs, microservices and service management

5. Appetite for major shifts and changes in organizational strength and structure.

Conclusion

Adaptability and anti-fragility

Businesses and enterprises in general, tend to be complex systems are their longevity and continued profitability depends on these systems being adaptive. An adaptive business is structured and enabled to build, design and offer products and services to their customers that are intelligent, intuitive and adaptive. This refers to the ability of the enterprise to consciously and subconsciously adapt to changing users, user preferences, user needs, operating environment, market environment and other relevant factors. Adaptability (think companies like GE and IBM) enables businesses to survive and grow.

In addition to adaptability, another interesting concept is that of anti-fragility. Anti-fragility is defined as the ability of a system to get better with an increasing amount of stress applied to it. Anti fragile systems are able to maintain their quality and resiliency even under stress and unknown or previously unseen factors.

Building products and services that are adaptive is easier compare to building products and services that are anti-fragile. Adaptive products and services are enabled to react to a certain definition of stress with a behavior that enables it to deal with that stress. Good product building has the ability to foresee such scenarios and react to it with a programmed response. However, building an anti-fragile system is much harder as it has to deal with scenarios that have been unseen so far and thus cannot be pre-programmed.

Artificial Intelligence and machine learning has the potential to make products both adaptable and anti-fragile by offering the analysis and organization of information to the product's workflow that is beyond human capability of comprehension and analysis. AI powered by compute, can be used to determine and detect subtle changes in consumer/user behavior and preferences and their expected outcome and can be used to adapt existing systems to the user's needs and plan/define new solutions to satisfy future needs.

Challenges to AI & ML adoption in product development

The main challenge in adoption of AI technologies is two fold. First, product teams need to understand that the development of an artificially intelligent system is very different from typical software development. Without digesting this point, product teams risk failing entirely in their initiatives. Symptoms of this disconnect can range from product teams expecting to "replace" key entire functions with AI to product teams expecting the AI driven system to perform at 100% accuracy.

Secondly, AI requires a retraining of almost the entire internal product delivery value chain (people, processes, products) to include the AI delivered value at key points in the value chain. Without understanding the impact of including and not including AI & ML driven insights at key points in the value chain, business run the risk of either completing missing the benefits of AI or mishandling the AI and unintentionally driving their users away along with their business.

The positioning of AI & ML enabled products is key to adoption. Initially, early in their journey, product teams should consider focusing on an "aid and assist" strategy as opposed to a "remove and replace" strategy. Earlier version of AI enabled systems should make users more productive, efficient and intelligent in their ability to meet and exceed their needs and tasks. This is not just important from a user needs perspective but key for the AI & ML enabled product to be able to "observe" the user and their behavior with and without AI & ML support to improve itself.

Consider the early adoption of self-driving cars. The concept is not new or recent as over the last few decades, slowly and steadily new enhancements such as "automatic braking systems" or "cruise control" have been paving the way for fully automated, self-driving cars. In the early phases, these technologies existed to "aid and assist" drivers while getting better in its ability to predict and adapt to changing road/pedestrian conditions.

The long term perspective

The world will see a huge impact from AI & ML being incorporated into all sorts of products and services. At the macro level, we will see a shift in how various industries and markets are organized. The speed to adopt AND deliver AI & ML enabled value will have a direct impact on the longevity and sustainability of the incumbents in all industries.

On the micro level, we will see a lot of activity through new products and services and enhancements in existing products and services that understand and predict the needs of the users and clients and AI-craft an experience that exceeds the expectations. A new class of Innovations driven by new patterns being detected in how complex markets and users function and operate will become common and products designed to leverage such patterns will be launched and delivered.

We can be sure that technology will progress to always determine the best path to reach the user's goals by analyzing and determining the best path to their goal through user observation, the user's past behavior, behavior of other users that resemble the user, the user's predicted future (professional and personal) and their currently used products. Consumers will demand and will be given products that know the user better than they know themselves and can offer the user an experience that is guaranteed to delight them. Similar to ABS and Cruise Control, users will be greeted with early innovations driven by AI & ML and not too far in the near future, users will look back and wonder why they wasted so much time driving around when they could have been driven around.